Also by Mary Jo Salter

POEMS

A Phone Call to the Future (2008)

Open Shutters (2003)

A Kiss in Space (1999)

Sunday Skaters (1994)

Unfinished Painting (1989)

Henry Purcell in Japan (1985)

FOR CHILDREN

The Moon Comes Home (1989)

NOTHING by DESIGN

The Soul Hovering over the Body Reluctantly Parting with Life
from *The Grave: A Poem* by Robert Blair, London, 1808;
engraving by Luigi Schiavonetti (1765–1810) after Blake

NOTHING by DESIGN

Poems by

Mary Jo Salter

Alfred A. Knopf · New York 2013

THIS IS A BORZOI BOOK
PUBLISHED BY ALFRED A. KNOPF

Library of Congress Cataloging-in-Publication Data

Salter, Mary Jo.
[Poems. Selections]
Nothing by design : poems / by Mary Jo Salter.
pages cm
ISBN 978-0-385-34979-6
I. Title.
PS3569.A46224N68 2013
811'.54—dc23   2013001009

Jacket images: (female northern cardinal) by John James Audubon, from
Birds of America. The Granger Collection, New York; (daisy and leaves) by
J. J. Rousseau from *La Botanique*
Jacket design by Jason Booher

Manufactured in the United States of America

First Edition

TO MY DAUGHTERS

Heavy in the womb,
at birth light as a feather—

not even your own mother
can understand that riddle,

or how you'd fill the room
although you were so little,

or how, once you had grown,
you weren't there to measure

yet stubbornly would loom
larger than anyone.

Contents

I

THE NUMBERS

MORNING MIRROR

He doesn't see me, whoever he is, who steps
through high grass in his khakis and bow tie
at six in the morning. I'm looking through the glass
of my cottage at the inn, hours before
coffee and buns begin at the conference.
He looks as if he knows things, and will speak
at his appointed time on experiments
successfully conducted, with a coda
on unforeseen, exciting implications,
and a call for further research. The wordless calm
of kayaks moored and mirrored, the yachts far off,
the silver-pink lake's lapping seem to please him.
He may be in a blessed state of non-thinking.
He runs a hand through thinning, tousled hair.

A witness at the window: somehow a deer
has sidled up, and is staring at me drinking
my coffee. I set it down, chastised. The same
plaintive and yet neutral gaze, as if
she knew once and is trying to recall my name.
I'm trying to unthink the expectations
of my given kind, to adopt another mode, a
curious but disinterested sense
of otherness. (Why is it for a week
all the deer have been either does or fawns?
Somebody knows the answer.) She wants more
from me, or maybe nothing; sniffs the grass,
nibbles a bit, then twitches: her profile high,
she bounds to the shore with leisurely, sure leaps.

PAIR OF BELLS

Joanna and Valerio
went up to the campanile
of the stone-deaf castle.

From across the courtyard, one
dented little bell with a skew
clapper could be seen.

I hadn't noticed the bellpulls.
But when Joanna yanked on hers,
and Valerio took his turn,

I heard a pair of louder bells,
deeper, surely bigger—though
these and both my friends remained

entirely invisible.
And the little bell, off-key
and out of sync, hung on and swung—

a third wheel like myself, moved
to celebrate a pair of bells.
Things happen but are parables.

COMMON ROOM, 1970

And Jesus said unto them, Come ye after me; and I will make you to become fishers of men.

—MARK 1:17

It was the age of sit-ins
and in any case, there weren't enough chairs.
The guys loped heavy-footed down the stairs
or raced each other to the bottom, laughing,
pushing their luck. But here they all crammed in,
sophomores, born like him in '51,
to huddle on the floor of the Common Room.

In a corner, a grandfather clock
startled the hour; hammered it home again.
He would remember that. The old New England
rickety dignity of the furniture.
The eminent, stern faces looking down
from time-discolored portraits. Or maybe some
of this was embellishment, added later on.

The flickering, thick fishbowl
of a TV screen, a Magnavox console,
silenced them all. There, in black and white,
gray-haired men in gray suits now began
to pull blue capsules from an actual fishbowl.
(At least the announcer said they were bright blue.)
It was the age of drugs. These looked like giant

Quaaludes handed out
by a mad pharmacist, whose grimly poised
assistant—female, sexless—then unscrewed
from each a poisonous slip of sticky paper.
A man affixed that date to a massive chart.
It was filling up already. (Some poor dude
named Bert was 7; he punched a sofa cushion.)

As for himself, he thought
of penny candy in a jar a million
years ago, picked out with his brother
most days after school. Or times he'd draw
tin soldiers from the bottom of a stocking.
(Born two days past Christmas, he'd always seen
that as good karma: the whole world free to play.)

A congressman was rifling
loudly through capsules, seized some in his fist,
dropped all but one. Not Jeremy? Good friend,
socked with 15. Two strangers, 38.
Ben got 120. Would that be good enough?
Curses, bluster, unfunny humor, crossed
fingers for blessed numbers that remained.

Somewhere, sometime in
that ammunition pile awaited his:
239. He heard the number whiz,
then lodge safe as a bullet in his brain.
Like a bullet in a dream: you're dead, you're fine.
No need to wish for C.O. or 4-F.
Oh thank you, Jesus God. No Nam for him.

Yet he was well brought up.
In decency, rather than dance for joy
or call up Mom right then from the hallway phone,
he stayed until the last guy knew his fate.
Typical Roy, who'd showed up late, freaked out
when, it appeared, his birthday got no mention.
He hadn't heard: they'd hosed him. Number 2.

Before the war was lost
some four years later, a handful in that room
would battle inside fishbowls, most in color—
and little men, toy soldiers in a jungle,
bled behind the glass while those excused,
life-sized, would sit before it eating dinner.
He'd lived to be a watcher. And number 2

in the Common Room that day?
Clearly not stupid. Roy became a major
in Independent Projects. Something about
landscapes in oil, angles of northern sun.
By the time he graduated, he had won
a study grant to paint in England, where
(so his proposal went) the light was different.

FRACTAL

A fish-shaped school of
fish, each individual
shaped like a single

scale on the larger
fish: some truths are all
a matter of scale,

in the manner that shale
will flake into thin layers
of and like itself,

or a roof is made
of shingle upon shingle
of roofish monad.

Scale, fish, school of fish . . .
"That's a fractal, isn't it?"
was your feedback when

you ate what I said.
"A form that's iterated:
output is input

ad infinitum."
Must I now mull it over?
I mulled it over.

This aquarium,
I thought, was a sort of think
tank for non-thinkers

in their open-mouthed
safety-in-numbers forage,
needing no courage.

Yet so beautiful:
mathematically serving
one end while swerving

in a fraction of
a second into action:
how do they sense when

to advance or back-
track, tail that guy, or swallow
the law to follow?

Somewhat in the line
of Leibniz, Mandelbrot coined
the term *fractal*: it's

the hall-of-mirrors
parthenogenesis of
a recursive, nonce,

anonymously
irregular form: i.e.,
copies no other

formula can make.
(I learned that when I got home.)
An eye on either

side of a flat head
is useful, I read; herring
have a keen sense of hearing,

but it's not that that
gives them their unerring
"high polarity,"

pooling together
just close enough to discern
skin on a neighbor,

far enough to skirt
collision. That's a vision
scaled for fish—but what

human can marshal
acceptance, much less a wish,
for sight so partial?

"Stand back from the glass,
make room for the universe,"
I thought then; "at least

for whatever we
can compass: iteration
on iteration,

until fish fill the ocean."

THE GODS

I always seem to have tickets
in the third or fourth balcony
(a perch for irony;
a circle of hell the Brits
tend to call "the gods"),
and peer down from a tier
of that empyrean

at some tuxedoed insect
scrabbling on a piano.
Some nights there's a concerto,
and ranks of sound amass
until it's raining upward
(violin bows for lightning)
from a black thundercloud.

A railing has been installed
precisely at eye level—
which leads the gaze, frustrated,
still higher to the vault
of the gilt-encrusted ceiling,
where a vaguely understood
fresco that must be good

shows nymphs or angels wrapped
in windswept drapery.
Inscribed like the gray curls

around the distant bald spot
of the eminent conductor,
great names—DA VINCI PLATO
WHITTIER DEBUSSY—

form one long signature,
fascinatingly random,
at the marble base of the dome.
It's more the well-fed gods
of philanthropy who seem
enshrined in all their funny,
decent, noble, wrong

postulates, and who haunt
these pillared concert halls,
the tinkling foyers strung
with chandeliered ideals,
having selected which
dated virtues—COURAGE
HONOR BROTHERHOOD—rated

chiseling into stone;
having been quite sure
that virtue was a thing
all men sought, the sublime
a mode subliminally
fostered by mentioning
monumentally.

All men. Never a woman's
name, of course, although
off-shoulder pulchritude
gets featured overhead—

and abstractions you might go
to women for, like BEAUTY
JUSTICE LIBERTY.

Yet at the intermission,
I generally descend
the spiral stairs unjustly
for a costly, vacant seat
I haven't paid for. Tonight
I've slipped into D9.
The lights dim. Warm applause

and, after a thrilling pause,
some stiff-necked vanities
for a moment float away—
all the gorgeous, nameless,
shifting discordances
of the world cry aloud; allowed
at last, I close my eyes.

A TOAST FOR RICHARD WILBUR

On the occasion of the fiftieth anniversary of his first book,
The Beautiful Changes

Poems like yours are, frankly, hard to beat—
    snapping and flapping from each line
    like a deceptively blank sheet
    that turns into an angel—but
    of course the image isn't mine;
your poems inspire the rest of us to cheat.

So, while I'm out borrowing, let me steal
    another angel from your brain.
    I'm thinking of Bruna Sandoval
    in your "Plain Song for Comadre,"
    who mopped the church floor seventeen
years, and daily saw her tinted pail

of scrubwater take the sheen of heavenly wings.
    For fifty years the beautiful change
    you've wrought upon the plainest things
    of this world has been like that—
    a private labor to estrange
the eye from yesterday, so that it brings

forward the clean habit of surprise.
    To become a "giver of due regard"
    you prayed to Saint Lucy once. I rise
    before you, glass raised, to insist
    that regarding you was never hard,
you for whom seeing is the keenest praise.

FROM A BALCONY, LAKE COMO

1.
Up close, last night's beads of rain
cling to the underside of the railing
like berries to a vine.

2.
Is it still raining? How to be sure
this morning, if not for the tall
columnar cypress

so many plummeting
meters down, a solemn
sentry standing at attention

to everything that can't be seen
by the human eye? Only
against such opacity

can we discern the soundless
drizzle, a mild
disturbance like midges.

3.
A blur of terra cotta
and ochre here and there:
while I describe it,

4.
the village is clearing a little.
Just below, a gardener's
broom of snapped branches

scratches a surface,
sidelines another heap of debris.
On a rooftop (so far from us

it's a floor), a roofer
plants his boots on the tiles,
fixing the middle distance.

5.
From which the village climbs again,
receding from
the valley in switchbacks

(we can tell because
of that minuscule vehicle
ducking in and out of trees)

to scale the face of the first
cloud-haloed
mountain in a series

of mountains, each slipped
neatly behind the last:
ever-flatter and -duller

file folders of color,
emerald to jade to a faded
wafer of blue so watery

it comes out of sumi-e.
A Japanese- or Chinese-
Italian scroll, a vertiginous

landscape hung
in the empty niche
between the open French windows.

    6.
When did the puddle
of rain on the balcony
chair disappear?

I thought I was looking.
Did it drip through the slats?
Evaporate? What?

    7.
Sun picks out
the young olive trees
positioned widely in a field

with their new shadows,
as if gawkily waiting
to be tagged in a game.

And on the lake, finally,
all agitations, tremblings
longed-for are visible:

slubbed yellows, prismatic
pinks like the costly
shantungs of Como

smoothed out on a counter,
cupped again, crumpled,
marveled at, lifted

to light; set aside.

    8.
Behind the brooding,
regrouping humidity,
lightning

is assembling all our
slate-blue, shifting
late afternoons into one simple,

zigzagged, single-minded line:
not here yet, but
coming on schedule

like the ferry pushing
off from Varenna,
appointed to veer this way.

CONSTELLATIONS

His parents want him to play less.
Well then, they should have thought ahead—
they *knew* the type of mind he had;
Dad never should have taught him chess.

But face it, Dad's still limited
at seeing long-term consequences.
Dumb strategies, those lame defenses—
it makes him sad, alone in bed

on a Saturday night, beneath a quilt
his mother calls a floral chessboard;
at only five years old, he'd floored
them both by beating him. (It's guilt,

not sadness, that he's really feeling:
he gets the picture faster than
they'll ever fathom.) Tonight again
he looks up at his stickered ceiling

for the vision of the infinite
Grand Master. There, instead of glue-on,
glow-in-the-dark stars, the view
some guys make do with, he has eight

squares by eight: a constellation
of white on black, a sixty-four-
tile universe, a dizzy dance floor
on which his moves, some combination

he thought of, might not have been seen
once in the game's unending annals.
King-usurping gambits, channels
around the wide skirts of the queen.

He should be "thinking about dating,"
his mother says. As if he isn't!
She seems to think he's self-imprisoned
here, that some brave girl is waiting

to rescue him, like Rapunzel, from
the castle. Of course he's desperate
to kiss them, to plunge into that sweet
wet something: but thinking hard can summon

even that sensation. It's long
since he has bothered clasping, lifting
a piece: admittedly, the shifting
of objects on a plane isn't wrong,

if you need that, but he's in a space
mentally where he needs no square
markers above him to know he's there,
sliding a checkmate into place.

How not resolve it, knight after knight,
side-sneaking bishop, stalwart pawn?
He'll probably be up till dawn
with this endgame—genius, if he's right—

but even when sleep's stubborn law
overtakes him, some new dream position
may break the surface: if not a win,
he thinks, at least a draw.

CARDINAL NUMBERS

Our heads down, two of a
kind, we're reading at either end
of the red sofa.

Is it a one in a million
chance? Not that such
a thing would happen—

that each of us
would look up to catch
on the wing that moment—

but that we speak in unison
when (framed in a mullion
of double windows)

two cardinals descend
to a fiery perch
on a barren pear tree.

Perfectly twinned,
they're content to stand
for pure ornament,

to be bright but dumb:
"like red bows
tied to the boughs."

That's what we both said.
Attachment is in
the air, evidently.

So we note, in tandem,
another twosome
mirroring them:

the marvelous,
upright, waxen ear-
trumpets of amaryllis

propped on the sill,
their double-bloomed red
deaf to the blaring

echo outside;
blind to the cardinals
that are blind to our staring.

Off the pair flies
to amaze somewhere else.
Our two pairs of eyes,

back and forth like birds,
flit from the plant
to twice-read words.

OUR FRIENDS THE ENEMY

Christmas 1914

Were they mad?
They kicked the severed head
of the football across the frozen mud
like Ajax running wild in the field:
it was sheep he killed
when he'd thought he'd been slaughtering
Odysseus and Agamemnon.

Now it was either the war to end
all wars, or Armageddon,
but surely they'd been out of their wits
picking their way across No Man's Land
unarmed but for brandy and cigarettes
and pictures of girls they liked.
In no time the chaps with cameras
were snapping photographs—
Tommy swapping his cap for the spiked
pickelhaube on Fritz.

It started, Colonel, the night before.
Sir, I can explain . . .
The Jerrys who wanted them dead so close
all along the front
they could hear them clear
as the stars, singing "Stille Nacht."
Some of the boys sang back:
"O Come All Ye Faithful."
A friendly taunt:

"Engländer! Engländer!"
And all ablaze,
the candles in rows
on the Germans' Christmas trees.

How did they dare walk across?
They'd trod their way through worse before—
lads underfoot in the muck;
now the day was cold enough those poor
contorted stiffs
were coated in merciful rime.

As for them, whose time
hadn't come, you could say that squalor
was the better part of valor.
You could call it a sort of luck
not standing in standing slime in the trench.
Not fraternizing with the rats
but clambering over the parapets
with a few of your rations in hand.

Sergeant Bernard Joseph Brookes
of the Queen's Westminster Rifles
wrote in his diary:
In the afternoon I went out
and had a chat
with our friends the Enemy.

And the football game?
It was a sort of courtship
before the first, last, passionate fusion.
Or it felt like the smiling sorrow

after you and your girl have split up.
But nothing forgiven, furious, tomorrow.

The Germans won, 3 to 2.

On Boxing Day
the mercury rose, and the mud.
It was agreed—
let the dead bury their dead—
and side by side, they dug.
They laid them in who hadn't played
but had already lost:

each a tidy Christmas package
tied with a cross.

II

THE AFTERLIFE

NORA

Even in death your radiance follows me.
Or leads me. You're ahead of me on the sidewalk,
pushing your baby's pram as I push mine,
and you swing your head to greet someone driving by,
your sheet of black hair the shiniest anyone
has ever seen; you don't even understand
that nobody in her thirties shines that much,

nobody laughs so musically at jokes
that are not that funny. Whatever it was I said
twenty years ago, whatever anyone said
no longer is heard, or can be, the way you took it
because you're not here to beam it back, to turn it
funny or beautiful—even the saddest things
you somehow made useful to us who were sad

with those infinite eyes of yours, looking right at us,
that *Oh* that was all acceptance. Even in death
that swept down upon you, death that locked you shut
and the *No* that is locked inside your name now, Nora,
I see the *Ra* for sun god, too, which is silly,
but you'd understand; I take it for your radiance
that even now in the darkness follows me.

THE AFTERLIFE

*Oh shabti allotted to me, if I be summoned or if I be detailed to
do any work which has to be done in the realm of the dead . . . you
shall detail yourself for me on every occasion of making arable the
fields, of flooding the banks or conveying sand from east to west;
"Here am I," you shall say.*

—BOOK OF THE DEAD

I.

They're looking a little parched
after millennia standing side
by side in the crypt, but the limestone
Egyptian couple, inseparable
on their slab, emerge from it as noble
and grand as you could ask of people
thirteen inches tall.

The pleasant, droopy-breasted wife
smiles hospitably in her gown
(the V-necked sheath "a style popular
for the entire 3,000-year
Pharaonic period").
Her skin is painted paler than his:
a lady kept out of the sun.
Bare-chested in his A-line kilt,
her husband puts his spatulate
best foot forward, so as to stride
into a new life.

Not mummies; more like dummies.
Not idols, yet not merely dolls.
Stocky synecdoches
of the ruling class, they survey
an entourage of figurines
at work providing necessaries
for long days under the reigns
of dynasties still unborn.

To serenade them, here's a harpist.
A dwarf even in life—
a mascot to amuse the court
whose music must not be cut short.
A potter modeling vessels that seem,
like him, already fired in a kiln.
Six silos of wheat,
imaginary granaries.
A woman of stone grinding grain,
as she would have, on a quern of stone.
A woman winnowing grain in a pan.
Another on her knees, kneading.
A brewer mashing a vat of beer,
a butcher slitting the throat
of a heifer for the hereafter.

2.

What had it felt like, that credence
in the afterlife of art?
To die, as the departed did,
comforted by the guaranteed
incarnation of a statuette;
to feed then on that slaughtered meat?

To take a leap from the stock-still
tyranny of the literal?
To see the miniature, the fiction
as a grow-in-the-dark depiction
of the soon-to-be actual?

3.

Aboveground, thought was evolving.
So many lords and ladies died;
not everyone could be supplied
with a finely sculpted retinue
of laborers to keep them living.

And how were the high ones to keep
so many minions at their task?
The overseer with his whip
became a smiling, bland convention:
one foreman for every ten or so
farmers with a hoe.

It wasn't only math.
Something unforeseen
was undermining transfiguration—
a canny, efficient faith
that less detail might well stand in
for the stand-in;
a simplicity of encryption.

Hundreds and hundreds of years passed.
Alabaster, faience, wood,
the scale of the factotum totems
dwindled as numbers multiplied;
jostled in the mass graves

of toy-box coffins, they were transported
by a procession of living slaves
a little distance, and slipped
into their niches in the crypt
for the shelf life of eternity.

Thumb-sized effigies wrapped
in bandages of holy script,
the hieroglyphed *Book of the Dead.*

Words. The nominal vow to work,
not the enactment of work.
The *shabti* held one stylized tool,
barely identifiable—
and were serene as Christian saints
with their hatchets and wheels, the instruments
of a recurring martyrdom.
In time they grew more mummiform,
cross-armed at the chest
or armless. Finally, curiously, at rest—

like zeros who were something
in being nothing,
place markers of their own
as much as of the master's soul.

    4.
And on the wall of a vault,
an artist has drawn himself—
or a cunning substitute—
at work, shaping a life-sized *shabti*
designed to be his twin:

a goateed dandy that our mute,
vainglorious ventriloquist
settles on one knee.

Profile to profile, they stare
into the mannered mirror
of one another.

In whatever kingdom this was
(by now, the blink
of one kohl-lined, almond eye),
what did people think was the life span
of the stunt man who betokens man?
The *shabti* sent to make *shabti*?

But the question too has shrunk,
eroded to vocabulary—
one fine old potsherd of a word
to be carried from the museum
like any other item
in the museum shop:
a replica necklace, a postcard.

The visitor is illiterate.
What did that stone scroll say,
meant to convert someday
to the thing it represents, papyrus?
Even the scribes couldn't read.
Something about the god Osiris
who came back from the dead.

She must be going.
Feels for the gloves in her pockets,
empty hands for her hands.

Opens a door to Chicago,
where a fine dust is ticking
coldly onto everything;
where she is still alive, and it's snowing.

IT'S HARD TO SAY

That's what you say a hundred times a day.
      Yet we keep asking.
("How was your morning? Did you like the nurse?")
The worse you get, the louder we keep asking—
as though, if you heard better, you could say.

Two adjectives bob up sometimes, depending.
      Good things you call "amazing."
("How was the garden? Did you like the birds?")
Things are either "terrible" or "amazing."
Nothing is in the middle. It's the ending,

the drawn-out ending, of your verbal life.
      "It's hard to say,"
you say, as though by thinking you'd remember
your sentence: word by word, still less to say.
This man here is your son. I am his wife,

and it is, indeed, terrible and amazing
      you must be told again.
I know *you,* though—that undimmed politesse
of eighty-plus years when, awestruck again
by a too-brilliant question, you sit there gazing

thoughtfully into space, and only then
do you say the terrible thing. "It's hard to say."

CITIES IN THE SKY

The buildings you drew were stooped
a little like you, lanky and tall and shambling
in your cloud-colored sweater, smiling vaguely
but curiously through your chic, black-rimmed,
perfectly round glasses.

Good morning. Yes thanks, coffee.
Show me your latest cities.
Or in any case, cities I can't keep straight.
They hunch and huddle in my head—
the toy building-block houses,
blank-faced and pink and red,
that fall willingly from some cliff you invented

but do not fall; they stall.
They stay there, falling; even you don't know why.
We drink more coffee in Claverack,
New York, on a day of arctic cold
and I inspect another high
cloud packed like an attic

with a city, clover-leafed with ramps
of cheerful, commuting cars, wherever
cars commute to up there,
a cloud that hovers like the dream
of the cows below,
unaware they're dreaming:

they're realists in their watercolor,
browsing, heads down, on a meadow
of saturated green.

Another cloud, jammed with people, is shaped
exactly like a map
of the continental United States.
"That's interesting," you say. "I didn't see that."

Thought clouds, that's what these are, as in
cartoons of characters thinking.
No words for what you're thinking, though,
just blueprints, unfeasibility studies, for cities
no one has time to build—

pulleys and sluices, ladders and cranes and pipelines
to nowhere. Bridges to caves. Nowhere
somewhere changing to something.
Knife-edged but bulging vehicles, cut
as from a tray of strudel.
A city sliced across the cranium,
its brains exposed like a motherboard.

Blockhead figures, only their bodies sinuous,
twisting like wind-whipped banners.
A robot stepping right through the plaster
walls of a town house,
leaving his empty shape behind
like a crumbling shadow.

Oh, here's your wife of fifty-some years,
the adorable Colette.
She has brought us farm eggs, juice, and toast.
Stay for a bit; your houseguest
has more to ask.

Is this what you think the afterworld is,
cities of real and unreal things
cohabiting in the sky?

That was only a question. I meant it idly.
Wake up, Jim, don't die.
It's only eight in the morning.

OVER AND OUT

Ladies and gentlemen, this is your captain speaking.
Those of you on the left side of the aisle
surely have spotted, on this fine Fourth of July,
fireworks erupting all around the city.
Pockets of color. Ooh baby, look at that.
From thirty thousand feet, you never hear
the *pop pop* when they open. No, they seem
to blossom in the dark, in suspended silence—
to dilate and fill like delicate parachutes
descending with curious tautness, until at last
they safely resolve to a shimmer of memory
that lingers like stars, then truly disappears.
Or that's what I'm seeing. Excuse the poetry.
Sometimes I get carried away up here.
I've left the seat-belt sign illuminated,
and though we expect no turbulence, weather-wise,
I'll ask you not to move about the cabin
unless you have to. The truth is we're in trouble.
Those of you on the right side may have noted
a funny rumble. That's not the fireworks, folks.

I'm going to get this plane down the best I can.
I bet you'd trade in every one of your frequent-
flier points for the real-life parachutes
we lack on this particular budget aircraft.
Wouldn't it be divine if we all drifted
to terra firma guided as if by winged
angels in parti-colored, ballooning silks?
Instead I'm duty-bound to propose that you

gather up—not your personal belongings
but any final reflections you may feel
will comfort you. Naturally you hate
being reminded your fate is in the hands
of faceless authority—that would be me;
but my advice is, try to rise above that.

You should have had a third little flask of scotch,
some of you are thinking. Some of you gals
are wishing our steward Keith, in business class,
so handsome, were available for a few
minutes, anyway. Triumphant sex
with strangers as the fireworks fade forever—

the dizzy thrill of The End? That dream would only
come true in the pathetic paperbacks
you brought on board. Real terror, let me tell you,
is no aphrodisiac. How stupidly
you lined up for this trip! How much you cared
who was preboarded first, or whether Misty,
our blonde in coach, would start from the front or back
when she rolled out her little tinkling cart
of snack boxes, which, although not fit for a dog,
you paid for meekly, and with the exact change.

Let's be frank. This flight is headed for
your longest vacation. Tonight, the only gates
we'll taxi to are pearly: no connection
to the party raging on down there without us.
It's far too late to squander precious seconds
resenting my sadly true banalities,
my jocular despair, my loud, phoned-in
philosophy no button can switch off.

I understand, though. You'd like a little peace
before the eternal one. Well, here you are.
Spend your last moments in big-hearted hope
we're going to hurt nobody on the ground.

III
....

UNBROKEN MUSIC

we drop everything to listen as a
hermit thrush distills its fragmentary,
hesitant, in the end

unbroken music.

—"A HERMIT THRUSH"
Amy Clampitt, 1920–1994

UNBROKEN MUSIC

1. *Lenox, 2007*
From an overlooked trunk
in your New England attic,
and bound in a week
for Lake Como, I happen

on your small, marbled notebook
from the same place, begun
the same week of May
sixteen years before.

At seventy-one
you'd have three years more.
Surely you thought
you'd have longer: spring

days to clean out
what you never meant,
or meant no one to read
(even us, the ring

of the last ones, the trusted
who sat at your bed).
But then, as you said,
in time everything

we save will be lost.
And who *could* read your scrawl—
like a lizard darting
from a stone wall?

2. *Rain at Bellagio*
Thunder wakes me:
electrical storm behind
the mountains but no
skeletal hand
of evidence, no rain, just a flash
of a dream and almost afraid
to look at it

I reach for the little book
I brought on the plane.
Open it and truly
read for the first time.
Crumbled like
crackers in bed, pressed
flowers I can't name

spill from the sheets
of dated poem-notes
5/21/91
moonlight on the wet flagstones
and the picayune
twin columns
of expenses

taxi $3.25
tip 50 cents
apportioned between yourself
and *H,* your lover
of decades by then.
Comically undomestic,
hopeless really, but ever

the Depression-era
Iowa farm girl so
haunted, so imprinted—
in sophisticated,
well-heeled, celebrated
old age—by the fear
of poverty.

I didn't fully know;
still now, surely,
have no right to. Guarded
in what you said
even in solitude, peevish
perhaps but decorous,
you've left here only

tantalizing scraps
of Jamesian prose:
To that towering pompous stick
of an academic
she has, Dorothy W.—like,
given up her life.
To wish them gone is so rude

that one resists it, and
becomes the more put off.
Oh, I can just hear you!
Did hear you, only today,
for the first time
in years, on my laptop
cleverly set up

to obliterate distance:
log on, double-click, play
audio: dead
distinguished poet
reciting in her proud,
high-pitched, breathy, not
entirely misremembered voice

a poem about the call
of a hermit thrush. Impossible
to achieve back then
the high-tech séance (yours
was the Italy
of the last *gettone*
jammed in the slot

of the bar's one phone,
the slow, shrugging Italy
of *francobolli*
licked for luck onto cards
destined not to arrive
at their destination). Radically
old-school anyway, you

traveled via the QE2
and your manual typewriter.
And your scribble
in journals: what terrible
penmanship, Amy, when
will you learn to correct it?
In loving memory

of Sidney . . . of Stanley . . . who?
A graveyard you visited
near here, apparently.
You took the time to
copy the epitaph
whole, and almost
wholly illegibly.

An hour has passed.
Three a.m. The storm's
now moving in on
the villa you stayed in
and pounding the moonless
flagstones. Static
hissing, a long-playing record.

   3. *The Horned Rampion*
Bookmarked—by violets, I think—
the page of field notes is itself
a plot of withered, once-wild jottings
to make sense of later *rockrose (pink)*
candytuft erinus alpinus

wood sage? cistus (shrub) nightshade
with tiny white clusters myrtle daphne
What's this then? *horned rampion*
Oh! it's her first thought for her last
enraptured botanical poem *a spiny,*

highly structured, blue-purple star
Phyteuma Bellflower family:
rare at first sighting, the rampion
would be rampant just days later. This
was the wildflower she'd plant

as if by happenstance at the end
of the poem, where a volume
of *Encyclopedia Britannica*
(frequent companion, from which whole
paragraphs were duly typed

and inserted into correspondence
she hoped was edifying) falls
open at random—was she lying
to get at something true?—upon
its genus, species, and illustration.

For her, the trouvé had been *old love
reopened* daring words *still quivering*
but who'd believe her notebook fallen
open to the seed of her poem
about another book fallen open?

　　4. *A Silence Opens*
Down at the lakeside, pleasure boats like toys
are glinting, tethered to their tinkling buoys

like spinning tops at last come to a stop
but for the slightest bobbing . . . as I've followed

my nose to scented hedgerows, ending here,
unable to botanize; can hardly tell

one boat from another. *Educata,*
one of them is called: I write that down,

absurdly, and with a heavy skeleton key
issued to the lucky ones like me

let myself out the gated come-and-go
Eden to Pescallo. A fishing village

sloshed at the margins, wind-and-grit-eroded
cobbles boldly throwing back the sun.

Chastening, and happily so, to stumble
like Alice (in your favorite book) upon

such rough, offhand perfection, facing page
of privilege, steep alleys flanked and straitened

by fitted jigsaw walls from which *fiori
spontanei* sprout sideways from the mosses

that seem to mortar one rock to another
in matrices, in story upon story. At a wrought-

iron gate, I glimpse it now: can see beyond
your phrase *truncated entrance to the olive*

groves of Pescallo whose mystery made me wish
you'd lived to finish, start, a poem about it.

What life isn't truncated, a path
that vanishes to a point of no perspective

upon itself again? The silvered heads
nod on the olive trunks; are ancient, wise,

indifferent as I turn to cross another
threshold of surprise just up the road:

the planted slabs of a little cemetery.
Come in. No gate, no lock, and as if these

lines were chiseled just for me: IN LOVING
MEMORY OF SIDNEY HERBERT BRUNNER

OF WINNINGTON CHESHIRE Look! AGED 23
WHO LOST HIS LIFE IN SAVING HIS ELDER BROTHER

FROM DANGER OF DROWNING Yes, this is the one
HIS BODY WAS RECOVERED and was tossed

the wreath WHITE FLOWER OF A BLAMELESS LIFE.
No wonder you had copied it all out

in spidery haste, the prairie poet drawn
time and again to drownings—of fishermen

in Maine; of the broken, heavy-lidded, stone-
pocketed Virginia Woolf, who blamed

no one; of Keats at twenty-five, whose lungs
filled with a choking liquid, and who called

out famously to erasure *Here lies One
Whose Name was writ in Water.* And here's the flip

side of serendipity (my guide
thus far): it's this, the accidental horror,

young life cut short, the petrifying thing-
not-supposed-to-happen. But what was?

You and I used to say there was no fate,
only "the coincidence factory," and so what

to make of this?—that our young hero's corpse
surfaced in 1890 on the date,

the very date, September tenth, when you
would meet your death in Lenox, a hundred four

years later? Nothing. Happenstance. As is
my coming on it, noting it, or opting

to remember him or you; to use my life
to set these words *still quivering* to paper.

    5. *Matrix*
After all that, you didn't quote it. Laid
poor Sidney so deep in your final book
that nobody reading *faceless in their nook*
outside the walls, the name and birthplace of
the Englishman who drowned there could unearth
a shard of identity. Homage instead
to wordlessness, to the silent, stubborn worth
not only of the forgotten but of forgetting.
I'm packing up. Taking a cue from love
as defined by you, or in a phrase of letting
go that itself was soon shucked off: *such*
infinitudes of things that lived—

                          So much
for them, a memory virus in our blood

that surfaces to scar us, disappears
awhile, is survivable. Who will trouble

to cobble together what we did or said,
how will they choose? Finally unable
to salvage one word more, I see ahead
only to Lenox, to returning all your green
thoughts to their resting place. Amy, where
could I pick your flowers, take up your *snakeskin*
of Eden left behind but in the fierce
desire to live my own days, light as air?

IV

LIGHTWEIGHTS

T. S. LIGHTWEIGHT AND EZRA PROFOUND

A meditation upon "The Waste Land"

Give Ezra his due credit
for that amazing edit.
Still, T.S. is the one who said it.

OUT OF THE WOODS

What is it about the forest?
Why can't we give it a rest?
All those writers taking
soulful walks in the woods:
good heavens, it's been done.
Step out and get some sun!
Dante did, after getting the goods
in the darkest glades from Virgil;
but what about Longfellow
sadly tagging along—
or ten steps back, at the distance
of a translated insistence?
Sure, I admire the flight paths
of the hawkmoths of Nabokov,
who pinned them down in a knockoff
of the hawthorn path in Proust—
but if I *must* lose my way,
I'll take the route of song:
give me Sondheim any day.
I've had my fill of Frost,
proud again to be lost,
coming upon his fork
in the road for the millionth time,
or stumbling upon woodpiles
of somebody else's work.

EDNA ST. VINCENT, M.F.A.

Chic and petite, blind to her destiny
of being hailed upon her death the worst
sometimes-excellent poet in history,
she ran the reading series, and ranked first
in her year despite some issues, namely those
pretentious, creaky sonnets e-mailed late
for workshop, densely wrought with "thee"s and "thou"s,
Apollo's "dewy cart," man's "frosty fate" . . .
Her classmates listened, bored, without a clue.
Still, they liked her, partly because she friended
everybody who asked, and fucked them too,
lending them each some notoriety
by blogging through the night how things had ended.
Plus, she knew people at A.W.P.

URBAN HAIKU

Leash dog; strap iPod
to bicep; jog, shower, dress—
it's not worth the time.

*

Thought at the checkout:
stupid to put five seltzers
in one plastic bag.

*

New leather jackets:
hand in hand, the married rich
strolling to MoMA.

*

Like an Olympic
torch held aloft: a steaming
latte with no lid.

*

What makes them do it—
jaywalkers in dark clothing
at night, in the rain?

*

Hailing a taxi—
finally one pulls over.
Proof I must exist.

DR. SYNTAX AND PROSODY

Ms. Martin at Princeton knows firsthand how electronic searches
can unearth both obscure texts and dead ends. . . . She recalled
finding a sudden explosion of the words "syntax" and "prosody"
in 1832, suggesting a spirited debate about poetic structure. But
it turned out that Dr. Syntax and Prosody were the names of two
racehorses.

"You find 200 titles with 'Syntax,' and you think there must be
a big grammar debate that year," Ms. Martin said, "but it was just
that Syntax was winning."

—*THE NEW YORK TIMES*
December 3, 2010

The sentence, diagrammed,
is a boring one-track course:
Dr. Syntax was a horse.

Prosody enjambed
himself near the finish line.
It happens. Hey, that's fine.

KITTI'S HOG-NOSED BAT

For some learned people
this creature, whose torso
(a bumblebee's size)
makes it smallest of all
the thousand-plus species
of bat on the planet,
and the most petite extant
species of mammal—
though some experts cite
the Etruscan shrew—

is worth a life's study.
Carry on, please do.

But others will care
only who Kitti was
and if he was teased
(as his name meant cat)
when he christened the hog-
nosed horrible bat.

I am numbered with these.
I'm not speaking for you.

FRENCH HAIKU

1. *Proust, Book One*
The elaborate
word ballet whereby Odette
turns into a Swann.

2. *Mont Sainte-Victoire*
Still-life tablecloth
heaped and crumpled: yet Cézanne
lets no stone roll off.

3. *Concierge*
Old and sort of fat,
she thinks she's sexy: yes, I
want to be like that.

OUR PING-PONG TABLE

Literary, lazy,
unsporty, unoutdoorsy,
and seriously unlikely
to reform our habits much,

we bought it feeling flush
one summer, and resolving
to have more family fun
than whatever we'd been having.

We read the warning: *Some
assembly is required.*
The very thought of that
made us cross and tired

but we put our heads together,
tore hunks of Styrofoam,
and built the big, "all-weather,"
eight-legged, hope-green wreck

while watching unmarked, tiny,
essential pieces sent
all the way from China
as placidly they went

irretrievably rolling
through slats in our old deck.
Nothing to do about it.
In a way, that was consoling.

How many years ago
was that? ten?—and how few
games did we play each year?
One day we stopped. But when?

I think I was the first
to notice poison oak
where the balls were prone to land.
After the net frame broke

we knew it was the end,
though there were nights we'd throw
a tablecloth or two
on top for a barbecue.

All-weather? So far it's stood
as a tottering monument
to the bumblers we remain;
it's stood there in the rain

and, through the kitchen window
in winter, as an efficient
means to measure snow.
I've liked that. That's been good.

INSTRUMENTAL RIDDLES

Nothing to shake a stick at,
hollow inside, I'm anything but shallow.
The deeper I am, the louder
silence is struck a blow.

drum

Love often looks like me—
two lovers, and then three—
although, in love, the third stays out of view.
I play upstage. I can be quiet, too.

triangle

I live on a limited scale.
Homeless, I collapse and wheeze
on the subway. As if you care!
Sorry to be so sentimental,
but buddy, please,
can you spare a dime?
Otherwise you may have to bear
the polka, one more time.

accordion

Shaped much like an angel's wing,
like angel hair my lengths of string,
I'm strummed by angels as they sing.

harp

In nursery school, before you learned to read,
you played like Pan upon a simple reed.
My name says what I do—
I bring your earliest memories back to you.

recorder

NO SECOND TRY

Why should I blame her that she filled my days
With misery . . .

               —W. B. YEATS, "No Second Troy"

Why should I blame him that he filled his days
With mistresses, or that he came home late
To meet most ignorant trust with smiling ways,
Such thoughtful gifts, and claims that I looked great—
Whatever that meant, though clearly not desire?
What help if I'd been wiser, with a mind
Simply to hurl his laundry in the fire
Rather than buy his tall tales with a kind
Solicitude and a deluded kiss,
Having cleaned his house from stem to stern?
Why, who else could he use, a guy like this?
Was there another wife for him to spurn?

V

....

BED OF LETTERS

I was angry with my friend:
I told my wrath, my wrath did end.
I was angry with my foe:
I told it not, my wrath did grow.

—WILLIAM BLAKE,
"A Poison Tree"

STRING OF PEARLS

The pearls my mother gave me as a bride
rotted inside.
Well, not the pearls, but the string.
One day I was putting
them on, about thirty years on,
and they rattled onto the floor, one by one . . .
I'm still not sure I found them all.

As it happened, I kept a white seashell
on my vanity table. It could serve as a cup
where, after I'd scooped the lost pearls up,
I'd save them, a many-sister
haven in one oyster.
A female's born with all her eggs,
unfolds her legs,

then does her dance, is lovely, is the past—
is old news as the last
crinkle-foil-wrapped sweet
in the grass of the Easter basket.
True? Who was I? Had I unfairly classed
myself as a has-been? In the cloister
of the ovary, when

released by an extra dose of estrogen,
my chances for love dwindled, one by one.
But am I done?

THE GAZEBO

It's my last day at the house.
My last time wandering the backyard.
I'm not aware I want to crush anything.
My boots crunch through the desiccated,
frosted grass, a sound like stubbing out
cigarette after cigarette.

I climb to the top of the hill
and unlatch the creaky gate in the fence
that frames the swimming pool.
I don't see it, but there's a crust
of ice beneath the canvas cover.
Plus algae, a few dead frogs and bugs,
however things stood last August.

Eons ago. Before I knew.
Another creaky door now, to the gazebo.
An icicle crashes from the roof
as I lower myself
into a plastic Adirondack chair.

Our view: three mountains, shy and local,
that spoke a little of yearning; of gratitude.
Mosquitoes got in through these screens.
And wasps would hover
near nests stuck to the beams and rafters
like harmless mischief; like wads of chewing gum.
There was laughter up here, iced tea, beer.
Paper-plate family meals, tête-à-têtes,
and silent reading alone, and sunsets

one shouldn't see alone. And a husband
who'd walk up and knock, a little joke,
before he'd let himself in.
I see him smiling. He asks how I am.
He's wrapped in a towel; he's been in the pool,
he's dripping on the floor, we chat,
we're the luckiest couple you've ever met.

But it's December. And the dripping now
is the sound of melting icicles
sharpening into knives.

DRINKING SONG

He lay with me upon a time,
sweet it was and lemon-lime.
Wedding ring and ringing bell,
Champagne was it never hell.

Coffee tea and morning toast,
none loved more and love was most.
Up we dressed for dinner out,
Prozac and Prosecco, doubt.

Peace in time and time to seethe.
Open wine and let it breathe.
Mix up our imperfect match:
dry martini, olive branch.

Jesus, who agreed the whore
he shall have with him always more?
Econo Lodge and Scottish Inn,
vodka, orange, scotch, and gin.

Years and years they met by day,
nights and nights forgot away
till the thing had not occurred.
Whiskey, whisper not a word.

What knows who was laced with truth,
shaken cocktail? Twist of ruth?
Panic and alarm creep back,
Ativan and Armagnac.

In my mind the slipping gears.
In our come-cries down the years
sometimes was love not sublime?
Another round, and hold the crime.

COMPLAINT FOR ABSOLUTE DIVORCE

A little something to endorse:
Download attachment, print and sign
Complaint for Absolute Divorce,

the lawyer wrote with casual force.
Yet why complain? The suit was mine.
A little something to endorse

"Complaint": sheer poetry, of course,
more lofty than Lament or Whine.
Complaint for Absolute Divorce:

so well-phrased, who could feel remorse?
That "Absolute" was rather fine.
A little something to endorse

the universe as is: for worse,
for better. Nothing by design.
Complaint for Absolute Divorce,

let me salute you, sole recourse!
I put my birth name on the line—
a little something—and endorse
the final word, then, in "Divorce."

BED OF LETTERS

Propped like a capital
letter at the head
of what was once our bed,

or like a letterhead—
as if your old address
were printed on my face—

I'm writing you this note
folded in sheets you lay
on then, but sleeplessly

night after night, a man
whose life became about
the fear of being found out.

Rarely a cross word
between us, although today
I see the printer's tray

of your brain, the dormant type
sorted in little rooms
to furnish anagrams,

fresh headlines, infinite
new stories in nice fonts.
Give her what she wants,

you must have thought, and brought
home seedlings to transplant
in flower beds, unmeant

to bloom into such tall
tales—which even you
can't unsay or undo.

And yet it's true that long
ago, two lovers dozed
naked and enclosed

one history between covers.
We woke and, shy and proud,
read our new poems aloud.

VI

·····························

THE SEAFARER

a version from the Anglo-Saxon

THE SEAFARER

I can sing my own true story
of journeys through this world,
how often I was tried
by troubles. Bitterly scared,
I would be sick with sorrow
on my night watch as I saw
so many times from the prow
terrible, tall waves
pitching close to cliffs.
My feet were frozen stiff,
seized and locked by frost,
although my heart was hot
from a host of worries.
A hunger from within
tore at my mind, sea-weary.

But men on solid ground
know nothing of how a wretch
like me, in so much pain,
could live a winter alone,
exiled, on the ice-cold sea
where hail came down in sheets,
and icicles hung from me
while friendly hall companions
feasted far away.
The crashing sea was all
I heard, the ice-cold wave.
I made the wild swan's song
my game; sometimes the gannet

and curlew would cry out
though elsewhere men were laughing;
and the sea mew would sing
though elsewhere men drank mead.

Storms beat against the stone
cliffs, and the ice-feathered
tern called back, and often
the sea-sprayed eagle too.

No kinsman can console
or protect a sorry soul.
In fact, a city dweller
who revels and swills wine
far from travel's perils,
barely could believe
how often, wearily,
I weathered the sea paths.
The shadows of night deepened,
snow fell from the north,
and on the frost-bound earth
hail fell like the coldest grain.
For all that, my heart's thoughts
pound now with the salt
wave's surging; on high seas
my spirit urges me
forward, to seek far
from here a foreign land.

The truth is that no man—
however generous
in gifts, however bold
in youth, however brave,

however loyally
his own lord may attend him—
is ever wholly free
in his seafaring from worry
at what is the Lord's will.

No, it is not for him,
the harp's song, nor the rings
exchanged, nor pleasure in women,
nor any worldly glory,
nothing but welling waves;
the longing of seagoing
man is what he has.
Groves break into blossom,

the towns and fields grow fair
and the world once more is new:
all of this spurs on
the man whose mind and spirit
are eager for the journey,
who yearns to steer his course
far across the sea.

Mournfully the cuckoo's
voice cries out in warning,
the harbinger of summer
bitterly foretells
in song the soul's distress.
To the wealthy warrior
blessed with worldly fortune,
this is all unknown—
what we face who follow
the vast and alien way.

And now my thought roams far
beyond my heart; my mind
flows out to the water,
soars above the whale's path
to the wide world's corners
and returns with keen desire;
the lone bird, flying, shrieks
and leads the willing soul
to the whale road, and over
the tumbling of the waves.

The joys of the Lord can kindle
more in me than dead
and fleeting life on land.
I do not believe the riches
of this world will last forever.
Always, without fail,
of three things one will turn
uncertain for a man
before his fatal hour:
sickness, age, or the sword
will rip the life right out
of the doomed and done for.
So it is for every man:
the best praise will come after,

from people who outlive him;
today, then, he must toil
against enemies and the Devil;
undaunted he must dare
so that sons of men extol him,
that in time to come his fame
endures amid the angels,

and his glory goes on, ceaseless,
among the celestial hosts.

The days are dwindling now
of the kingdoms of this earth;
there are no kings or Caesars
as before, and no gold givers
as once, when men of valor
performed great deeds and lived
majestically among
themselves in high renown.
Their delights too are dead.
The weakest hold the world
in their hands, and wear it out
with labor, while all splendor,
like the earth, grows older;
its noble aspect withers
as man does everywhere.

Age creeps up on him,
his face grows pale; his head,
gray-haired, bewails old friends,
sons of princes, already
given to the earth.
As his body fails,
life leaks away, he tastes
sweetness in things no more,
nor feels pain, nor can move
his hand, nor use his mind.
When a kinsman dies, he wants
to strew the grave with gold,
or bury with the dead
treasures he amassed.
But no, it cannot be;

gold once hid and hoarded
in life is no good now
for the soul full of sin
before the force of God.

Terrible and great
is the Lord, and the very world
turns from Him in awe.
He made the firm foundations,
the earth's face and the heavens.
Foolish is he who does not fear
his Lord; death comes to him
though he is unprepared.
Blessed is he who lives in all
humility; what comes to him
in Heaven is forgiveness.
God gave to him that spirit
to bow to all His power.
A man must steer his passions,
be strong in staying steady;
keep promises, be pure.
He must be wise and fair
with foes as much as friends,
well-tempered in himself.
He dreads to see a dear one
engulfed in flames, yet patience
tells him to trust the sway
of Fate, and that God's might
is greater than we know.

Let us ponder where our true
home is, and how to reach it.
Let us labor to gain entry

into the eternal,
to find the blessedness
of belonging to the Lord
joyfully on high.
Thanks be to God who loved us,
the endless Father, the Prince
of Glory forever. Amen.

VII

LOST ORIGINALS

VOICE OF AMERICA

I sit at my desk
My life is grotesque.

—JOSEPH BRODSKY

    1. *Open to the Public*
Hard labor? But you'd claim it wasn't hard.
You sat in your log cabin, ably sketching
another cabin, and some chickens scratching
out their appointed living in the yard.

A farmhand reading poems by kerosene,
you plotted carefully the coup d'état
of yourself, and boiled another cup of tea;
a well-turned sentence made you feel serene.

I sit in Russia's National Library,
rifling through folders of your private stuff.
They came easily—or not easily enough,
illiterate as I am in the very

language which to you was the first god.
Your faintly ruled, cheap spiral notebooks hatched
fresh images, new chickens came unlatched
from their coop, and from a corner, a man's head—

a twenty-something profile. That was yours.
You doodled, and you knew your keepers well.
You studied English, though you couldn't spell;
you daydreamed in unguarded metaphors.

Well, here's one for you, touching and grotesque.
After you died, a citizen of the States,
they shipped some furniture of yours in crates
to Petersburg: your velvet couch, your desk—

actually two of them—from your South Hadley
room and a half. Or so your house had seemed,
those maple floors as slippery as in the dreamed
Leningrad apartment; brightly, sadly,

you'd write your parents, who had watched you jammed
into a taxi, snapped in a photograph,
and lost forever. Your desk sent *here*? I'd laugh,
if it were funny, studying a framed

Madonna and child, a cat, a Mandelstam,
an Auden; a pocket-sized address book, still
open to the last call; your manual
typewriter, outdated as a ham

radio no one again can operate.
The last icon is you. Incredible.
That's you in tuxedo tails, with your Nobel,
in a video that loops as if your fate

had always been a hero's. Applause and cheers
repeat on the TV screen within a house
that once was your old friend Akhmatova's:
hero without a poem for years and years.

2. Tears at the Fountain House

Out in the garden, where for years her spies
chain-smoked while she sat indoors and nearly starved,
an art show. Wine and cheese are being served.
Today's the opening, and a viewer's eyes

are free to interpret anyhow, it appears.
Hung as if on cobwebs, or on memories
of traumas left unspoken, from the trees
giant water balloons droop like the tears

in your poetry that welled and wouldn't land.
(Your mother told you weeping was for grave
occasions: obedient, you were brave.)
Don't touch the tears. I brush one with my hand,

stroll about the grounds, and though I doubt
you'd love the installation, you'd round up
some artsy types—high-booted girls and hip
boyfriends in ripped jeans—and ask them out

to a smoky bar nearby, if you were here.
But you never will be. Never came back to grill
the next generation, shame them, crush their will—
or that's how your taunts and teasing, your severe

quizzing came off, exiled to the warm
and fuzzy American classroom. Coeds cried.
You shrugged and tried again: identified
lines where native speakers missed the poem.

"Ms. Salter? Andrew Marvell. Tell the class."
I heard my heart pound loudly in my head.
Tell them what? Declaim "An Horatian Ode
upon Cromwell's Return . . . " perhaps? What an ass

I was—or maybe you were; I wasn't sure.
Now it occurs to me: the poem of his
to recite into these flower beds would be less
"The Garden" than the twining "Eyes and Tears,"

where "all the jewels which we prize," he wrote,
"melt in these pendants of the eyes"; and "happy they
whom grief doth bless, that weep the more, and see
the less." Lovely; but the tears stayed in the throat,

or were meted out in rhyming drops of ink.
Lament was Russian, roughly; in the English
of Marvell, Hardy, Frost, you got your wish
for irony's containments. You could think.

   3. *Border Crossing*
You had them in your head—Pushkin, Gogol,
Dostoevsky. Best memory I ever met.
Nobody learns by rote now; quotes come out
from under the patchwork overcoat of Google—

a development you'd have found unnerving,
at least until you found some figure for it.
In Venice, you wrote, "a gigantic china teaset"
was heard vibrating when church bells were serving

"on a silver tray" their peals to the "pearl-gray sky."
Your mind, a gondola on the lagoon
of time, skimmed the reflections in your own
outlandish, errant, metaphysical eye,

as if everything in the world could be amassed
on a single page in white with words in black,
although a tear might drop to it, a "throwback,
a tribute of the future to the past."

Somebody boarded up, because they could,
the door from your parents' room to yours. Or yours
to your parents'; but to me it hardly matters:
the living border crossing to the dead

is what I'm after. I stepped onto a plane
because I could, and joined your friend who'd taken
snapshots of your departure; though I'm shaken
to be standing in their one room—mute and plain,

erased of bed and table, of evidence
of birthday parties, songs at the piano,
piled-up cups and saucers, the radio
from which state "drivel" flowed like water once—

I don't need much, only to turn and walk
down warped linoleum in the communal hall
where the black phone still cowers on the wall,
to see you—overheard—pick up and talk.

4. Watermark

The Foundation's conference room. Tea and coffee,
biscuits, sugar, brisk handshakes, respect,
and quick interpreters for the select
Americans invited to a country

some of us know little of. Academician
Likhachev, they tell us, would have liked
to meet us all. *Your fellowships, in fact,*
our conversations here, were his late mission,

he whose life would closely coincide
with the twentieth century; who bore the stamp
of public servant, scholar, and of camp
prisoner. A miracle he hadn't died

at Solovki, where he heard three hundred gunned
down as he hid, three hundred on the dot—
he was to be among them, but was not,
which meant that someone else . . . The thought-of sound

reverberates on walls washed with the sun.
This was his radio. Mid-century relic,
midsized, ordinary, somehow orphic.
Likhachev marked it—see the painted line

dripping down the tuner? That's the Voice
of America. Others marked the BBC.
This was a sign we wanted you to see . . .
The hardened teardrop holds its frequency.

ENGLISH COUNTRY DOLLHOUSE

Which scholar among the dolls
that stepped out from this room
(in volume, like one volume

of the *O.E.D.*)
needed spectacles?
A wire-rimmed, folded pair—

like a glossy insect
crushable in one swat—
lies lenses-up, not seeing

but wanting to be seen
as a letter, a giant *B*
for *Book,* upon a tiny,

leather-bound, gilt-edged tome
in which the words must be
unthinkably minute.

Are there really words in there?
The book, after all, is shut.
If I could step through the glass

of the museum case,
I'd shrink myself to fit
in that empty chair and put

those glasses on—whereby
I'd know whatever it was
I needed to magnify.

CRUSOE'S FOOTPRINT

*At last he lays his head flat upon the ground, close to my foot, and
sets my other foot upon his head, as he had done before; and after
this made all the signs to me of subjection, servitude, and submission
imaginable, to let me know how he would serve me so long as he
lived.*

—DANIEL DEFOE, *Robinson Crusoe*

*The poet who writes "free" verse is like Robinson Crusoe on his
desert island: he must do all his cooking, laundry and darning for
himself.*

—W. H. AUDEN

And Elizabeth Bishop did it, in her "Crusoe
in England": though she needn't have scanned a foot
in writing it, every step was itself alone
and demanded whatever served. Sometimes she cast
her thought in sestinas; found at her typewriter keys
to set free memories otherwise confined,

or labored within a villanelle to find
lost houses, continents, like the geometer Crusoe,
whose world to map had no scale and no keys;
who saw the surf wash in, efface his foot-
print like a sandpiper's. The melted cast-
les of sand we've made are in the end all one:

what company we have when we feel alone!
A solitary stroll on the beach to find
ourselves rewards us, largely due to the cast
supporting us from the wings, the backstage crew so
handy, the believable props, and the foot-
lights revealing the beaming spectators: keys

to our happiness, in which the fashionable quais
Auden wrote of slosh with talk about us alone.
We're not, in fact, entirely sorry for the foot-
note-in-mouth disease of the critics who find
what was never there in two-dimensional Crusoe.
Surely he would have liked to attend the cast-

away party that followed him—the downcast,
austere "Robinson" poems of Weldon Kees
the suicide, or *Émile* by that crank Rousseau,
who thought he'd bring up a boy on Defoe alone.
Swiss Family Robinson? There: we've defined
the branching tree-house of writing. Friday's foot

is at his master's head, and at the poet's foot
the subject's breathing: admittedly these are caste
systems, and guilty as charged, we the jury find.
No man is an island; we're more like the Florida Keys—
a stanza of lines that each began alone.
Whoever free-floats, it isn't versatile Crusoe,

who cast his dreams with people he hoped to find,
and through years without lackeys, never slept alone
given the draft at his foot, his *Robinson Crusoe.*

LOST ORIGINALS

All his life he spoke of "lost originals," as if he were reaching beyond
his own civilization to the simplicity and grandeur of a remote
past . . .

—PETER ACKROYD, *Blake*

The window to the mortal world
shows mountain islands in the sea.
One of them rises at the same
slope the soul floats from the body

flat on the bed, in stony folds,
the profiled head propped on a pillow.
A second distant hill has curled
into a corner of the window

(more a mirror than a window)
precisely in the size and shape
of the other pillow at the foot
of the bed from which, now flying up

from feet of clay, utterly free,
the female soul looks down on man,
her weeping hair a kind of pity,
her breasts as round as sun and moon.

*

For a pittance he would illustrate
the poems of others, like *The Grave*
by Robert Blair (forgotten now,
of the graveyard school). He would engrave

a scene like this to make ends meet,
or sometimes furnish a first sketch
for wretches like that Schiavonetti—
who wrecked this one, and couldn't etch—

but beauty in the end was his,
for right was left, and black was white,
the world was flat and he went round
his cottage blessed with second sight,

like Catherine, his better half,
and when the visions would forsake
both of them, "What do we do then, Kate?"
"We kneel down and pray, Mr. Blake."

                    *

Soul peeled like a printer's proof
off the body's copper plate.
Hands black as a chimney sweep's
worked and with black hands he ate.

Raging at injustices
to all of humankind, yet placid,
steady with needle, burin, paint,
he brushed the pastel tones with acid.

The worldly took their patronage
elsewhere when he made them wait
for pages queerly old and new,
ahead of their time, and always late.

Time was of such little note!
Heaven came by *the infernal*
method, corrosives, which in Hell
are salutary and medicinal;

birds sang their eternal song
and angels lodged beneath his roof.
Off the body's copper plate
soul peeled like a printer's proof.

      *

Illuminations like stained glass
on paper, or like parasols
that shaded with a pale translucence;
enlightenment from Paracelsus

himself, beloved sage, who said
imagination is like the sun:
its light, intangible, may set
a house afire. O let light in

from deities of every source—
the New and the Old Testament,
gods of the Greeks, the Romans, Norse,
gods of *wise heathens,* gods that went

so many eons back he had
to invent them, so to mourn their loss.
Saturated colors sang
prophecies. In *The Song of Los*

he burned the institutions, *Churches:*
Hospitals: Castles: Palaces:
(built, he wrote, *like nets & gins*
& traps to catch the joys

of Eternity) on a treated plate
and turned it, coining true from false.
"All his life," the future wrote,
"he spoke of 'lost originals.' "

              *

London turned meanwhile, cog-wheeled
industry of speed; grinding
people up in mills, it spilled
William Blake on common ground.

Rest in peace, white chalk and red,
hammer and chisel, rest in peace,
aqua fortis, vinegar,
salad oil, and candle grease.

No gravestone for the great engraver.
Never mind. We'll meet hereafter.
Catherine, who'd lost her beauty
to toil and hunger years before,

had posed a last time (*you have ever*
been an angel to me), and
sold his works to stay alive.
Let the future understand

he sat with her for hours together
daily following his death,
and she followed his instructions
from Jerusalem or Lambeth,

Bunhill Fields, Soho or Felpham,
Fountain Court, all was the same—
and soul, its twisted sheets in tatters,
rose up from its bed of letters.

Acknowledgments

A number of artists' residencies helped me greatly in writing this book. I am grateful for a Bellagio fellowship from the Rockefeller Foundation, and for several stays at the MacDowell Colony, one of which was supported by a Concordia Foundation fellowship. A period as a Director's Guest at Civitella Ranieri, as well as visits at The Whiteley Center, gave me time and peace to write.

My thanks to the editor of this book, Deborah Garrison, and to the editors of the following magazines and anthologies, where these poems appeared for the first time, sometimes in slightly different form.

The Atlantic: "Out of the Woods"; *The Common:* "The Gods"; *The Cortland Review:* "Instrumental Riddles"; *Five Points:* "Cities in the Sky" and "Our Friends the Enemy"; *The Hopkins Review:* "Common Room, 1970," "Fractal," "Our Ping-Pong Table," "Over and Out," "Pair of Bells"; *Little Star:* "French Haiku," "Nora," "Voice of America"; *The New Yorker:* "Complaint for Absolute Divorce"; *The Plume Anthology of Poetry:* "Edna St. Vincent, M.F.A."; *Poetry Northwest:* "From a Balcony, Lake Como," "It's Hard to Say," "Lost Originals," "Unbroken Music"; *Sewanee Theological Review:* "Dr. Syntax and Prosody"; *Southwest Review:* "The Afterlife"; *Subtropics:* "No Second Try"; *3QR: The Three Quarter Review:* "Crusoe's Footprint"; *The Yale Review:* "Constellations"; *The Warwick Review:* "Cardinal Numbers." "The Seafarer" appeared first in *The Word Exchange: Anglo-Saxon Poems in Translation,* edited by Greg Delanty and Michael Matto (Norton, 2011).

Dedications

"Morning Mirror" is for Ann Hulbert; "Pair of Bells" is for my friends at Civitella Ranieri; "Common Room, 1970" is for David Brown; "Fractal" is for Daniel Hall, Pengyew Chin, and Kannan Jagannathan; "The Gods" is for Stephen Kampa; "From a Balcony, Lake Como" is for Jean McGarry; "Cardinal Numbers" is for Emily Leithauser; "Our Friends the Enemy" is for Albert and Janet Salter; "Nora" is in memory of Nora Kornblueh; "The Afterlife" is for Hilary Leithauser; "It's Hard to Say" is in memory of Gladys Leithauser; "Cities in the Sky" is in memory of James Rossant; "Over and Out" is for John Irwin; "Unbroken Music" is for Karen Chase and Caolan Madden; "Edna St. Vincent, M.F.A." is for Joseph and Carla Harrison; "Dr. Syntax and Prosody" is for Greg Williamson; "French Haiku" is for James Magruder and Stephen Bolton; "Instrumental Riddles" is for Claudia Emerson; "Crusoe's Footprint" is for Mark and Bryan Leithauser; "Lost Originals" is for Gjertrud Schnackenberg.

A NOTE ABOUT THE AUTHOR

Mary Jo Salter was born in Grand Rapids, Michigan. She was educated at Harvard and Cambridge, and taught at Mount Holyoke College for many years. She also served as poetry editor of *The New Republic*. In addition to her six previous poetry collections, she is the author of a children's book, *The Moon Comes Home,* and a coeditor of *The Norton Anthology of Poetry.* She is Krieger-Eisenhower Professor in The Writing Seminars at Johns Hopkins University and lives in Baltimore.

A NOTE ON THE TYPE

The text of this book was set in Requiem, created in the 1990s by the Hoefler Type Foundry. It was derived from a set of inscriptional capitals appearing in Ludovico Vicentino degli Arrighi's 1523 writing manual, *Il Modo de Temperare le Penne*. A master scribe, Arrighi is remembered as an exemplar of the chancery italic, a style revived in Requiem Italic.

Composed by North Market Street Graphics, Lancaster, Pennysylvania

Printed and bound by Thomson-Shore, Dexter, Michigan

Designed by Betty Lew